AF270505

FOCUS ON FORMULA ONE

THE BEST MOMENTS OF
FORMULA ONE

BY ANTHONY K. HEWSON

SportsZone

An Imprint of Abdo Publishing
abdobooks.com

abdobooks.com

Published by Abdo Publishing, a division of ABDO, PO Box 398166, Minneapolis, Minnesota 55439. Copyright © 2024 by Abdo Consulting Group, Inc. International copyrights reserved in all countries. No part of this book may be reproduced in any form without written permission from the publisher. SportsZone™ is a trademark and logo of Abdo Publishing.

Printed in the United States of America, North Mankato, Minnesota.
052023
092023

Cover Photo: Mario Renzi/Formula 1/Getty Images
Interior Photos: Bernard Cahier/Hulton Archive/Getty Images, 4, 6, 14, 22; Jacques Boissinot/The Canadian Press/AP Images, 8; Mark Thompson/Getty Images Sport/Getty Images, 9; Darren Heath/Hulton Archive/Getty Images, 10; GP Library/Universal Images Group/Getty Images, 15, 18, 24; Pascal Pavani/AFP/Getty Images, 16; Pascal Rondeau/Allsport/Getty Images Sport/Getty Images, 20; Harry Melchert/Picture Alliance/Getty Images, 21; Joe Portlock/Formula 1/Getty Images, 26–27; Cristiano Barni/ATP Images/Getty Images Sport/Getty Images, 29

Editor: Charlie Beattie
Series Designer: Michael J. Williams

Library of Congress Control Number: 2022949090

Publisher's Cataloging-in-Publication Data

Names: Hewson, Anthony K., author.
Title: The best moments in formula one / by Anthony K. Hewson
Description: Minneapolis, Minnesota: Abdo Publishing Company, 2024 | Series: Focus on formula one | Includes online resources and index.
Identifiers: ISBN 9781098290733 (lib. bdg.) | ISBN 9781098276911 (ebook)
Subjects: LCSH: Formula One automobiles--Juvenile literature. | Automobiles, Racing--History--Juvenile literature. | Sports car racing--Juvenile literature.
Classification: DDC 796.72--dc23

TABLE OF CONTENTS

Juan Manuel Fangio consults with a crew member at the 1957 German Grand Prix.

CHAPTER ONE

GREAT COMEBACKS

The key to winning the 1957 German Grand Prix came in practice. Juan Manuel Fangio's Maserati team noticed that the tires on his car were wearing out early. While its Ferrari rivals opted not to stop to change tires, the Maserati team practiced its pit stops so they could change very quickly. Maserati got its stops down to about 30 seconds, a fast time in that era of Formula One.

However, the team's first pit stop did not go well. The strategy left Fangio nearly one minute behind the Ferraris. The Argentine had time to catch up, but he needed the drive of his life.

Fangio was already one of Formula One's biggest stars. But this was his finest hour. Fangio set lap records on each of his last 10 laps as he chased the Ferraris down. Even his seat coming loose on the final lap didn't slow Fangio down.

In the end, Fangio managed to win by 3.6 seconds. It proved to be the last race of his Formula One career. Fangio's nickname was *El Maestro*, "The Master." Of his 24 all-time

Fangio's win in Germany wrapped up his fifth drivers' championship in six years.

Formula One victories, the 1957 German Grand Prix was certainly among Fangio's best.

ON THE BUTTON

More than five decades after Fangio's amazing comeback, another driver had his own race for the ages. Englishman Jenson Button made an error in the 2011 Canadian Grand Prix that dropped him into 15th place early on. Then came rain and a two-hour delay.

When the race resumed, things went even worse for Button. He got a flat tire and fell to last place. But some other drivers struggled to decide between rain tires and regular tires during pit stops. Button stuck with intermediate tires, which gave him better traction than regular tires but didn't drag as much as rain tires. He quickly made up ground. Button weaved his way up through the

Heavy rain was just one of the problems Jenson Button had to overcome at the 2011 Canadian Grand Prix.

field, slowly picking off places until he was fourth with 15 laps left.

With five laps to go, Button was second. His car was running faster than leader Sebastian Vettel's, but it wasn't going to be easy to get around the German. Vettel blocked Button's every move. Finally, Vettel went wide in a turn and left space for the Englishman. Button darted past Vettel and went roaring into first. From that point on, Button never looked back.

It was one of the unlikeliest wins in racing history. Button later called it the best of his career. And it was proof that anything can happen on a Formula One track.

Button celebrates his unlikely victory at the 2011 Canadian Grand Prix.

Lewis Hamilton navigates the British Grand Prix's Silverstone track as heavy storm clouds loom overhead during the 2008 race.

CHAPTER TWO

INSPIRATIONAL MOMENTS

The 2007 season was a special one for Lewis Hamilton. The English driver burst onto the scene as a rookie and nearly won the title. As Formula One's only Black racer, he was a pioneer in the sport. Hamilton had also made a lot of fans at home who loved to cheer for the next great British star.

Fans were naturally thrilled to see him race on home soil at the 2008 British Grand Prix. Even the rainy weather didn't keep them away. The wet conditions made the race tricky—for some drivers. But Hamilton had grown up racing on the

A CLOSING PUSH

Jack Brabham entered the last race of the 1959 season at the United States Grand Prix locked in a tight championship race with Stirling Moss and Tony Brooks. By the last lap, it was clear that Brabham was going to win the title. Brooks didn't run the race, and Moss's car had dropped out due to mechanical problems. Brabham was in the lead, but then his car ran out of fuel. Wanting to finish any way he could, Brabham hopped out and pushed the vehicle the final 400 yards (366 m) over the line.

same track. He felt right at home.

Hamilton started the race in fourth position. However, he had launched himself into second by the first turn. It took him only five laps to claim his first lead.

Meanwhile, other drivers were struggling just to keep their cars on the track. The wet conditions had them all mixed up. But Hamilton was flying as if the track were perfectly dry. Even his own team started to worry and asked him to slow down. Hamilton did not. He knew how fast he could push the car while still staying in control.

Hamilton went on to win by over a minute in one of the most impressive drives in Formula One history. The spectacular race helped propel him to his first championship later that year. It was just the start of a legendary career.

LAUDA'S RETURN

Formula One has seen many great comebacks on the track. But Niki Lauda's best comeback didn't happen during a race. The fact that Lauda even got in his car for the 1976 Italian Grand Prix was truly remarkable.

The Austrian was a beloved racer, one of the most popular drivers in the sport. But a fiery crash at the 1976 German Grand Prix nearly ended his life. The accident left him badly burned. Many did not expect Lauda to survive due to all the smoke he had inhaled. Everyone thought his career was over.

Amazingly, just 42 days later, Lauda was back in the seat of his Ferrari. Pale, scarred, and in need

Niki Lauda prepares for the race before his dramatic return at the 1976 Italian Grand Prix.

Lauda finished 19.4 seconds behind race winner Ronnie Peterson at the 1976 Italian Grand Prix.

of tighter seat belts for all the weight he'd lost, Lauda had no fear in returning to racing. After some slow early practice times, Lauda quickly regained his speed.

At the Italian Grand Prix, the home race for Ferrari, Lauda managed a fourth-place finish. It was not the winning pace he'd established earlier in the year, but it was a stunning return to racing. Lauda went on to finish second in the world championship that year. By 1977 he was a champion again.

Ayrton Senna, *left,* embraces his teammate and racing rival, Alain Prost, *right*.

CHAPTER THREE

RACING RIVALRIES

Frenchman Alain Prost and Brazilian Ayrton Senna were two of the greatest drivers in racing history. Their careers overlapped in the 1980s, and the two often found themselves vying for the world championship. That led to one of the most intense rivalries the sport has ever seen.

What made the rivalry even more fierce was that the drivers were teammates. Their McLaren team was dominant, and they were easily the two fastest cars on the grid. In 1988 Senna had won the drivers' championship, but Prost was in the lead late in 1989.

The Japanese Grand Prix was the second-to-last race on the schedule. Senna needed a win badly. He led most of the way, but Prost made a late charge with six laps left. Suddenly the cars collided, and both went spinning off the track. Senna got his car going again and rejoined the race, but Prost was out. Senna went on to win and tighten up the title race.

Senna, *front*, and Prost, *rear*, dominated Formula One in the late 1980s and early 1990s.

However, race officials later said that Senna missed some of the track in rejoining the race. He was disqualified and had no way to catch Prost. One of the sport's greatest in-season rivalries ended in a thrilling and controversial fashion.

DRAMA DOWN UNDER

Just a few years later, another fierce rivalry was brewing on the track. Rising star Michael Schumacher had already gotten in trouble during the 1994 season for ignoring race rules. The German was banned for two races. But he still entered the season's final race with a one-point lead over his main rival, England's Damon Hill.

At the season finale in Australia, whoever finished higher between Schumacher and Hill would win the title. Schumacher led for much of the race. On lap 36 of 81, he brushed the wall.

Damon Hill, *left,* chases down Michael Schumacher, *right,* early in the 1994 Australian Grand Prix.

Schumacher recovered and continued, but Hill saw an opening to pass. The cars then collided, with Hill launched onto two wheels before going headfirst into the wall.

Both race cars were too damaged to continue. Since neither racer could finish, Schumacher was the champion. Many around the sport thought Schumacher had caused the accident on purpose since he knew it would keep Hill from winning. But an investigation called it a "racing incident" and cleared the German racer of any blame. The controversial win launched Schumacher's record-setting career that saw him win seven titles. Hill would have to wait until 1996 to win his first and only championship.

Schumacher celebrated his first season title after the completion of the controversial 1994 Australian Grand Prix.

Peter Gethin competed in only 30 Formula One races over his four-year career.

CHAPTER FOUR

LAST-LAP DRAMA

Some races, such as Lewis Hamilton's British Grand Prix win in 2008, are decided by minutes. Others come down to the final lap. But races don't get any closer than the 1971 Italian Grand Prix.

The race was exciting well before the finish. It featured 25 lead changes. Entering the final lap, five drivers had separated from the pack. Swedish driver Ronnie Peterson had a narrow lead over England's Peter Gethin. Right behind them were Mike Hailwood of England, New Zealand's Howden Ganley, and Frenchman François Cevert.

Gethin's tight win at Monza was the only time in his Formula One career he ever led a lap in any race.

Gethin had started 11th but moved up slowly throughout the race to challenge for the lead. Peterson didn't expect Gethin to test him at the end. But on the last lap, Peterson went too wide in a turn and left an opening.

Gethin roared through it and into the lead. Both cars tore down the final straight toward the finish line, chased by the other three contenders. As they crossed the finish line, Gethin shot his hand straight up in the air in triumph. He had won, but just barely. His margin of victory over Peterson was just .01 seconds—the closest finish in Formula One history. Cevert was just .09 seconds behind the leaders, while Hailwood finished .18 seconds back and Ganley .61 seconds. To anyone watching, the five cars appeared to cross the line almost on top of each other.

The dramatic win was the first and only one of Gethin's career. The 1971 Italian Grand Prix may not have determined any champions, but the tight finish remains legendary.

VERSTAPPEN'S VICTORY

A race that comes down to the last lap is thrilling. Even more exciting is a season that comes down to the final lap. That was the case in 2021 as both Lewis Hamilton and Dutch driver Max Verstappen

Max Verstappen, *right,* passes Lewis Hamilton, *left,* on the final lap of the 2021 Abu Dhabi Grand Prix.

dueled for the title. The two superstars were tied for first heading into the last race of the season. The title showdown took place in Abu Dhabi, United Arab Emirates.

Hamilton led a close race over Verstappen until a late crash behind them changed everything. The safety car had to come out to lead the cars slowly around the track while the wreckage was cleared.

HAMILTON THE HERO

Lewis Hamilton was on the other side of a dramatic last lap during his championship-winning 2008 season. Hamilton entered the season's final race, the Brazilian Grand Prix, in a tight race with Brazilian driver Felipe Massa for the title. Massa won the race, meaning Hamilton had to finish at least fifth to claim the season title. Hamilton passed German Timo Glock on the race's final corner to finish fifth and beat Massa by one point.

By the time the cleanup crew was finished, only one lap of full-speed racing remained to decide the title.

Verstappen had newer tires. When the cars went racing again, he closed in on Hamilton, looking for a place to pass. Finally, he made his move at Turn 5 of the 16-turn track. Verstappen gained quickly on Hamilton and lunged to the inside of the turn. He cleared the four-time defending world champion and launched into the lead. There was no looking back. Verstappen held on to win his first world championship.

Organizers later determined that the restart had not followed the rules correctly. The process change had probably helped Verstappen. Either way, it made for a thrilling finish to one of the closest Formula One seasons ever raced.

Max Verstappen is hoisted up by members of his Red Bull racing crew after his last-lap win at the 2021 Abu Dhabi Grand Prix.

GLOSSARY

disqualified
Made ineligible for a prize or for further competition due to violations of the rules.

drivers' championship
A title that is awarded each year to the Formula One driver who earns the most points throughout the racing season.

grand prix
From the French for "grand prize," any race that is part of the Formula One championship series.

grid
The full field of drivers in a race.

pit stops
Stops during a race to change tires or make repairs to a car.

rival
An opponent with whom a player or team has a fierce and ongoing competition.

rookie
A professional athlete in his or her first year of competition.

safety car
A nonracing car that leads the field around slowly when there is a dangerous situation on the track.

MORE INFORMATION

BOOKS

Hewson, Anthony K. *The History of Formula One*.
Minneapolis, MN: Abdo Publishing, 2024

Hustad, Douglas. *Innovations in Auto Racing*. Minneapolis,
MN: Abdo Publishing, 2022.

Rule, Heather. *GOATs of Auto Racing*. Minneapolis, MN:
Abdo Publishing, 2022.

ONLINE RESOURCES

To learn more about Formula One's
best moments, please visit
abdobooklinks.com or scan this QR code.
These links are routinely monitored and
updated to provide the most current
information available.

INDEX

ABOUT THE AUTHOR

Anthony K. Hewson is a freelance writer originally from San Diego. He and his wife now live in the San Francisco Bay Area with their two dogs.